FORCES AND MOTION
at work

Shirley Duke

ROURKE
PUBLISHING
www.rourkepublishing.com

www.rourkepublishing.com

PHOTO CREDITS: Cover: © Barbara Helgason; Title Page: © Viatcheslav Dusaleev; Pages 2,3: © Agsandrew; Page 4,5: © Goldmund, Shane Quentin; Page 5: © Jakub Krechowicz, Jstudio; Page 6: © gmnicholas, Tito Lessi; Page 6,7: © Ronald Van Der Beek; Page 7: © Wikipedia; Page 8: © Raycat, Chris Fisher; Page 8,9: © Fernando Rodrigues, Adventtr; Page 10: © Merzavka, ermingut; Page 10, 11: © Goldmund; Page 11: © Paul Fleet; Pages 12,13: © Goldmund, Sashkinw; Page 14: © Soldeandalucia; Page 14,15: © Goldmund; Page 15: © KrivosheevV; Page 16: © Juriah Mosin; Page 16,17: Goldmund; Page 17: © Teri Intzegian; Page 18,19: © Brad Thompson, Goldmund; Page 20: © VLIET; Page 20,21: © Goldmund; Page 21: © Nutthawit Wiangya, Jim Mills, Frederic Prochasson, Elena Elisseeva, Melissa King, Sandra Cunningham, Suzanne Tucker, ensup; Page 22: © natulrich, Roxana Gonzalez, Songquan Deng, Vereshchagin Dmitry, Songquan Deng, Joao Virissimo; Page 22,23: © Goldmund; Page 23: © Ratchanida Thippayos, Narcis Parfenti, Craig Barhorst, Gevorg Gevorgyan, Denis Babenko; Page 24,25: © Goldmund; Page 25: catscandotcom, YinYang; Page 26: © rocketegg, Page 26,27: © Goldmund; Page 27: © ActionPics; Page 28: © nem0fazer; Page 28,29: © Goldmund; Page 29: © ZU09, Teri Intzegian; Page 30: © Cynthia Farmer, Edgaras Kurauskas; Page 30,31: Tom Schmucker; Page 31: © Alejandro Duran, Vivid; Page 32: © Konstik, Yuri Arcurs; Page 32,33: © Goldmund; Page 33: © Jabiru; Page 34: © Aeronaut88; Page 34,35: Goldmund; Page 35: © Blueee; Page 36: © Seesea; Page 36,37: © Goldmund; Page 37: © Teri Intzegian; Page 38: © Martin Mann, Paul Topp, Nuttakit, Page 38,39: © Goldmund; Page 39: © Roman Borodaev, Sergey Suhanov, Sergey Bedniy, Sergey Gorodenskiy, Michael Goffin, Andrjuss Soldatovs; Page 40: © Maliketh, Goldmund; Page 41: © Goldmund; Page 42: © Stephen Sweet; Page 42,43: © Goldmund; Page 43: © Valery Kharitonov, Olga Khoroshunova, Goldmund; Page 44: © Oleksandr Pasichnyk, seamartini, Daniel Korzeniewski, srebrina, Sally Wallis; Page 44,45: © hypermania, Page 45: © Martin Vonka, ampower, Rafa Irusta Machin, ramblingman, freeteo; Page 46,47: © Goldmund

Edited by Precious McKenzie

Cover design and page layout by Teri Intzegian

Library of Congress Cataloging-in-Publication Data

Duke, Shirley
Forces and Motion at Work / Shirley Duke.
    p. cm. -- (Let's Explore Science)
Includes bibliographical references and index.
ISBN 978-1-61741-788-7 (hard cover) (alk. paper)
ISBN 978-1-61741-990-4 (soft cover)
Library of Congress Control Number: 2011924834

Rourke Publishing
Printed in the United States of America, North Mankato, Minnesota
060711
060711CL

www.rourkepublishing.com - rourke@rourkepublishing.com
Post Office Box 643328 Vero Beach, Florida 32964

Table of Contents

CHAPTER ONE

Unseen Forces

Climb aboard a roller coaster and hang on! It jerks and rattles to the top of a slope. It hovers a second before plunging into a stomach-thrilling drop. The turns sling riders from side to side. A jolting stop **forces** everyone backward. The ride is over.

The thrill of a roller coaster ride comes from the different forces acting on your body as the coaster changes directions and its velocity, or the speed, it is moving.

All these motions are forces. Forces are actions that start, stop, or change the shape or motion of a body. Early scientists, called **natural philosophers**, noticed patterns of motion between the Sun and Moon and the changing seasons. They asked questions and tried to explain their world.

Galileo studied motion in the late 1500s. He dropped objects of different weights from a building. He discovered that objects fall at the same rate. Until then, people believed heavy things fell faster than light ones. Galileo's discovery energized and upset scientific and religious communities.

$$\frac{F}{ma} = \frac{F}{ma}$$

FORCE
= Mass x Acceleration

F: resultant force measured in newtons (N)

m: mass measured in kilograms (kg)

a: acceleration measured in meters per second (m/s2)

Was Galileo Wrong?

Galileo dropped two objects off a tower. Try dropping a book and a sheet of paper. Do they hit the ground at the same time? They don't. Was Galileo wrong? Not at all!

A sheet of paper has more air **resistance**. That slows its fall. Heavy objects are not as affected by air resistance as light ones. Do the experiment in a vacuum—where there's no air. They'll hit the ground at the same time.

Try the experiment again. This time, place the paper on top of the book. Let go. Do they fall at the same rate? The book removes the air resistance. They should hit the ground at the same time.

Sir Isaac Newton studied nature in the late 1600s. He wondered why the Moon moved and never fell because he knew that when ordinary objects fell they always hit the ground.

Newton believed the same force that pulled objects down might be the same force that pulled the Moon. He defined this force as **gravity**, the unseen force holding the universe together. Newton's laws of motion and gravity came from his interest in the Moon.

Isaac Newton
1643-1727

Newton said all objects have **mass**. Mass is the amount of matter in something. Mass stays the same. Everything with mass exerts, or applies, a force on every other thing. Small masses exert less force so the force isn't as noticeable.

Mass is different from **weight**. Weight is defined as the force of attraction between a person and place in the universe. Weight can change, depending on the location.

On Earth, a person has a set amount of mass. Their weight is in pounds (or kilograms) and will change if they leave Earth. On the Moon, that same person has the same mass, but their weight is less. The smaller-sized Moon exerts less gravitational pull on their mass. The Moon's mass is less, so its gravitational pull is less.

Gravity exists between any two objects in the universe. With more mass, a body has a stronger pull.

What Would You Weigh on Other Objects in Space?

Ever wonder what you might weigh on Mars or the Moon?

Here's your chance to find out. If you weigh approximately 100 pounds (45.5 kilograms) on Earth, this is what you would weigh on different objects in space.

MOON
YOUR WEIGHT IS
16 lb. (7.3 kg)

THE SUN
YOUR WEIGHT IS
2,707 lb. (1,230.5 kg)

EARTH
YOUR WEIGHT IS
100 lb. (45.5 kg)

MARS
YOUR WEIGHT IS
38 lb. (17.3 kg)

Planets with large masses have a strong gravitational pull. The force a person exerts on a planet is small. A planet's huge mass holds people to the ground.

Distant bodies exert less gravitational pull. The Sun is too distant to pull people to it. Smaller bodies exert less pull. That's why people don't fall toward other people.

Newton's ideas introduced the science of **mechanics**. Mechanics is the study of forces and motion. The same force that pulls things toward Earth also pulls on things out in space. The Moon would go off in a straight line without Earth's gravity.

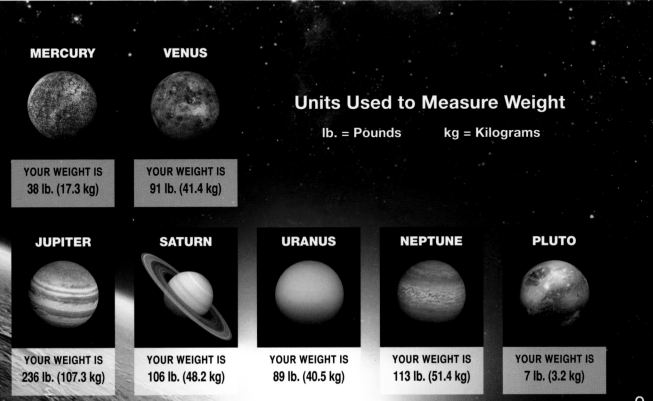

MERCURY • **VENUS**

Units Used to Measure Weight

lb. = Pounds   kg = Kilograms

YOUR WEIGHT IS
38 lb. (17.3 kg)

YOUR WEIGHT IS
91 lb. (41.4 kg)

JUPITER

SATURN

URANUS

NEPTUNE

PLUTO

YOUR WEIGHT IS
236 lb. (107.3 kg)

YOUR WEIGHT IS
106 lb. (48.2 kg)

YOUR WEIGHT IS
89 lb. (40.5 kg)

YOUR WEIGHT IS
113 lb. (51.4 kg)

YOUR WEIGHT IS
7 lb. (3.2 kg)

Magnets create another unseen force. Moving electric charges create a magnetic field. This force pulls materials like iron to it. Some materials are naturally magnetic. Other materials become magnetic by transferring the charges from another magnet.

Magnets have north and south poles. The electric charges line up in the magnet to make the poles. Like poles repel and opposite poles attract.

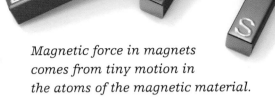

Magnetic force in magnets comes from tiny motion in the atoms of the magnetic material.

Electricity creates a magnetic field when charged particles flow through a wire coiled around iron. This is an **electromagnet**. Shut off the current, and the iron is no longer a magnet.

Earth creates a magnetic field from its molten iron core. The forces are strongest at the poles. Sunspots also cause magnetic fields.

An electromagnet is easy to make. All you need is a battery, insulated copper wire, and some iron, such as a nail. After you make your electromagnet, test it so see if it works.

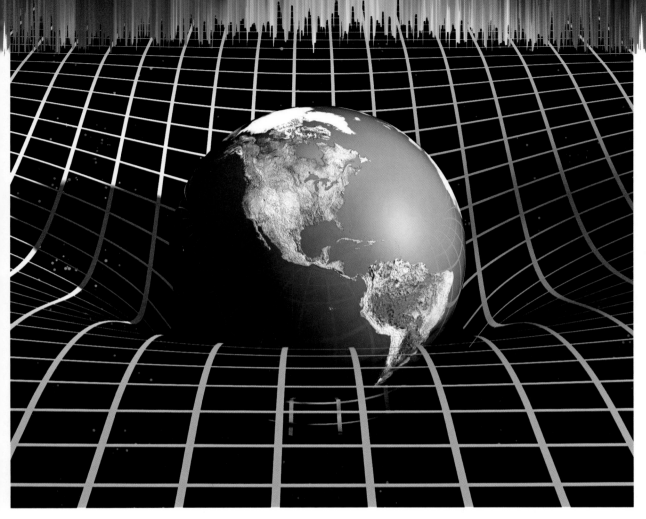

Einstein showed that heavier objects warp space, making objects with a smaller mass slip toward the depression instead of traveling through space on their course.

Albert Einstein's famous equation of relativity says matter makes space curve. He saw space and time as a flowing stream. This flow bends if an object disturbs it. Larger masses change the shape of space. This disturbs small masses, and moves them toward the large ones. However, this happens only near the speed of light.

Einstein identified forces exerted by atoms. He called them **nuclear forces**. Now scientists use early studies of motion and Einstein's ideas to help explain the motions and forces on Earth and space.

11

CHAPTER TWO

The Laws of Motion

Sir Isaac Newton studied motion, too. He noticed that moving things behaved in certain ways. He stated three laws to describe them.

Newton's First Law

The first law of motion states a body at rest tends to stay at rest and one in motion tends to stay in motion—unless acted on by an outside force. To change, an outside force must push or pull the object to make it move or stop.

The tendency of an object to keep moving or to stay at rest is **inertia**. If a ball rolls down the street, the tendency is to keep rolling. If it hits a rock, the force of the ball slams into the unmoving force, or the rock. The ball either stops or turns due to the force.

The force of the bowling ball hitting the pins depends on the mass of the ball multiplied by the acceleration, or how hard it is thrown. This is an example of Newton's second law.

13

A ball sitting on the ground must have a force directed at it to start moving. Without a force, inertia holds it still. A force must accelerate it, changing the speed or direction it moves.

A rolling ball won't keep rolling forever, even without hitting something. It stops because forces act on it to make it stop. Friction is a force made by two objects moving past one another. All surfaces have tiny ridges and bumps. These bumps and ridges resist motion. Objects hit the ridges and slow down. So the ball stops. This is because friction acts on it.

Without friction, this soccer ball would roll forever after you kicked it.

Newton's Second Law

The second law of motion gives a formula for acceleration. Newton's second law says the force (F) needed to accelerate an object is equal to the mass of the object (M) multiplied by its acceleration (A). The formula is written as: F = M x A.

The bigger the object is, the harder it is to get moving. It takes more force to accelerate something big like a car than it does to get a soccer ball moving.

Sonja's car, which weighs 2204 lbs. (1,000 kgs), is out of gas. Sonja and her friends are trying to push the car to a gas station. They make the car go 0.05 mph (.08 kmh). Using Newton's second law, can you compute how much force is applied to the car?

Newton's Third Law

Something with more mass has more **resistance**. Resistance opposes, or resists, the outside forces working on it. Push a tennis ball. Then push a bowling ball. The same force works on both balls. The tennis ball is easier to push. It has less mass than the bowling ball. The greater mass of the bowling ball takes more force to get it moving.

Newton's third law is about forces as actions and reactions. This law says for every action that happens there is an opposite and equal reaction. Recoil, the backward push after an action, shows this third law.

The further back the arrow is pulled , the greater distance it will travel. This is Newton's third law in action.

When a cannon fires and the cannon ball hurls forward, the force of the firing pushes the cannon backwards. In the past, cannons on ships were mounted on wheels. The reason the cannon didn't fly backwards off the ship like the cannon ball is because the cannon's mass was greater than the cannon ball. The force that moves the cannon back is equal to the force of the flying ball.

Another way of looking at recoil is in a rocket. The fuel in a rocket pushes down on the ground at a specific force. The same amount of force from the burning fuel pushes the rocket into the air.

Newton's explanations about gravity and motion advanced scientific thinking. But he didn't write about energy. In later years, other scientists studied energy.

WHAT'S IN A MODEL ROCKET?

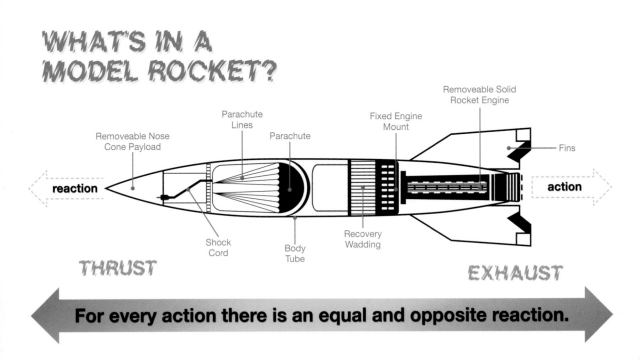

For every action there is an equal and opposite reaction.

CHAPTER THREE

Energy and Motion

Energy is the ability or potential to cause change. It measures how much **work** one object does when acting on another. Picture a soccer ball in the grass. It has energy because it can do work if a force pushes it down the field.

Energy can never be created or destroyed. It only changes forms. The Law of Conservation of Energy states that no energy is lost when it converts, or changes, forms.

Before the soccer ball is kicked, it holds potential energy. A force must act on it to make it release the kinetic energy.

Energy changes occur constantly. Grass uses light energy from the Sun. It converts the energy into food during the process of photosynthesis. When a cow eats grass, the energy is changed again. This time, the plant energy changes to chemical energy in the cow's body when the food is digested. This chemical energy from the food changes to physical energy when the cow walks to the barn using its muscles. The amount of energy remains the same, but with each change, more and more energy is lost as heat, so less energy is available after each conversion.

Energy from the Sun flows through the food chain from producers to consumers.

All forms of energy are either potential or kinetic. **Potential energy** is energy in a stored form. It does work if released. Chemical, gravitational, mechanical, and nuclear energy are forms of potential energy.

Kinetic energy is energy in motion. A box sitting on a table holds potential energy. Push it off the table and gravity pulls it down. This action changes potential energy into kinetic energy. Let's learn a little more about different types of kinetic energy.

Forms of Energy

POTENTIAL ENERGY

CHEMICAL
Chemical energy is stored in connections of atoms and molecules.
**Batteries, biomass, petroleum, natural gas, and coal are examples of chemical energy.

GRAVITATIONAL
Gravitational energy is stored in the height of an object. High, heavy objects hold more of this energy.
**Hydropower works from the height of water behind a dam falling to a lower level.

MECHANICAL
Mechanical energy is stored in the tension, or tightness, of an object.
**Heavy machines and wind up toys use mechanical energy.

NUCLEAR
Nuclear energy is energy in the nucleus, or center, of atoms. It holds huge amounts of energy.
**The Sun makes heat and light by nuclear reactions.

KINETIC ENERGY

ELECTRICAL
Electrical energy is electrons moving, usually through a wire.
**Lightning is electrical energy that doesn't move in a wire.

HEAT
Heat, or thermal energy, is the motion of molecules in a substance. They move faster as they heat up.
**Geothermal energy is heat energy from deep in the Earth.

LIGHT
Light energy is electromagnetic energy in light, infrared, X-rays, and radio waves.
**Sunshine is an example of radiant light energy.

MOTION
Motion energy comes from moving objects. An example is the blowing wind.
**Blowing wind is an example of motion energy.

SOUND
Sound energy is the movement of waves through substances.
**If there is no substance, a sound can't be sent or heard.

Kinetic Energy - Sound

Sound is kinetic energy that is usually measured in decibels. Decibels are a measure of pressure and intensity. Some sound waves have a very high frequency that we can't hear. These sound waves are called ultrasound waves. Ultrasound waves have many uses including medical tests, cleaning delicate instruments, and testing metal for cracks and flaws.

How Loud is it?

city traffic
(**85db**)

Hearing sounds above 90 decibels can damage your hearing over time.

washing machine (**75db**)

hair dryer, ((**90db**))

normal voices in conversation (**50db**)

whisper (**20db**)

0   10   20   30   40   50   60   70   80   90

Kinetic Energy - Electrical

Electrical energy comes from charged particles moving, most often in a wire. Electricity runs many appliances people use daily. Lightning is electrical energy. It's strong, so it doesn't stay in one place. It moves between the ground and the charged clouds.

A bolt of cloud-to-ground lightning can contain up to one billion volts of electricity. That's a whole lot of energy!

rock concert
(((**110db**)))

ambulance
(((**120db**)))

shotgun
(((**165db**)))

rocket launch
(((**175db**)))

100 110 120 130 140 150 160 170 180 190

Kinetic Energy - Electromagnetic

Electromagnetic energy is radiation made of waves and particles. It includes visible light waves, X-rays, gamma rays, radio waves, ultraviolet radiation, radar, and microwaves. They travel in a sideways direction. Each kind of energy causes different actions.

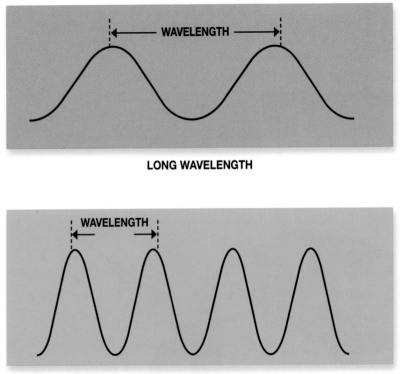

LONG WAVELENGTH

SHORT WAVELENGTH

Radio waves are the longest—which is 300 feet (91.44 meters), the length of a football field. Microwaves are about the size of an insect. Infrared and visible light are so small they can't be seen as waves. X-rays and gamma waves reach atomic sizes.

Kinetic Energy - Heat

Heat energy is energy transferred in moving, bouncing particles. Thermal energy is heat. It includes geothermal energy from inside the Earth.

Einstein showed that mass can be a form of energy, too. But this happens at the speed of light. Most changes aren't taking place that fast!

Hot springs are formed from superheated water coming from deep inside the Earth. The color in the hot springs comes from heat-loving microorganisms called thermophiles.

Kinetic Energy - Motion

Motion energy is in moving objects. The energy is released when the object slows. Wind is motion energy. A car crash is another example. The energy is released when a car hits something else.

This car was using motion energy until it crashed into something. Can you describe what happened after the car accident?

Properties of Energy and Work

Not only does energy change forms, it is constantly moving. Most forms are passed along by particles in waves. Visible light waves are the colors in the rainbow. Waves that can't be seen also move energy. Ultraviolet waves can sunburn our skin, but their waves are too short to see.

Work takes energy. Work is the amount of energy needed by a force to change it. Work is equal to the force exerted on the object, multiplied by the distance.

Think about pushing a bookcase. If someone pushes against a bookcase and it doesn't move, there is no work done. The person pushing might get tired, but the bookcase must move for this motion to be considered work.

Every day, people use energy and change its form to do work. But other forces act on motion and energy. What can forces do?

work = force x distance

How many different types of work are happening in this image? What would happen if number 50 tackled the player with the football?

CHAPTER FOUR

Changes in Force and Motion

Friction is a force that resists motion. This resistance changes mechanical energy to heat energy. Friction makes it harder to do work. It's also a problem in machines. Parts rubbing against other parts cause them to become overheated and wear them down.

Lubricants like oil and grease reduce friction. They make surfaces smoother. Ball bearings reduce friction, too. Only a small part of the round ball bearing touches the moving part at all times. Hovercrafts glide over water on a cushion of air. This reduces the friction.

Friction helps people grip the ground when they walk. Walking on ice reduces friction. Without friction, it's hard to walk. Writing takes friction, too. Pencils must rub against paper to make a mark. Friction helps light a match. Car tires grip the road to go around curves.

Friction in air is called air resistance. **Aerodynamics** is the study of how air flows. Race cars are designed to let air flow over them to reduce friction so that the race cars travel faster. The shape of the wings on airplanes lifts the plane into the air. To create lift, air must turn. The curved part of the wing makes the air turn.

Daniel Bernoulli
1700-1782

Bernoulli's principle helps explain lift, or why airplanes fly. The curve in the top of the wing makes the air flow faster over the wing creating low pressure. The air under the wing moves slower creating high pressure. This creates lift.

Bernoulli's Principle

CROSS SECTION OF AN AIRPLANE WING
Fast Moving Air = Low Pressure (above the wing)
Slow Moving Air = High Pressure (below the wing)

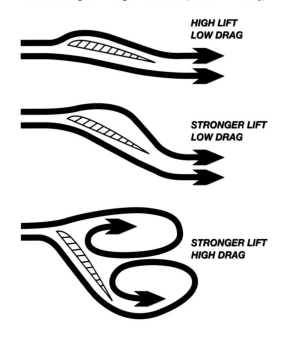

HIGH LIFT
LOW DRAG

STRONGER LIFT
LOW DRAG

STRONGER LIFT
HIGH DRAG

Aerodynamics is at work in many unexpected places. Streamlined bicycles reduce friction for riders. The bike supports are curved to improve air flow. Special tires reduce air friction.

A pitcher creates spin on a baseball to change the position of the ball over the plate. Beach balls, kites, and rockets use aerodynamics to move into the air.

Water friction is called drag. Boats in water pull some water along with them when they move. This water rubs against the rest of the water, causing friction. Friction increases as the boat goes faster. Streamlined boat shapes reduce drag.

Swimmers reduce friction by wearing streamlined swim suits. Some even shave their hair to reduce drag. Every second counts in the Olympics!

Can You See the Spin?

The hull, or underside, of a boat is shaped to fit the boat's use. A V-shaped hull cuts through rough water and makes the ride smoother.

Water is dense and even a little motion creates drag. To swim faster, streamline the body and reduce extra splashing when swimming.

When a pitcher throws a baseball, the spin turns the ball. This creates a force on the air moving around the ball. Depending on which way the ball spins, the pressure is reduced above or below the ball. This keeps the batter on his toes because he must see the spin to know which way the ball might move. A clockwise spin lifts the ball. A counterclockwise spin lowers the ball.

Pressure also changes forces exerted over an area. Feet sink in deep snow because feet are small. Put on skis and a person stays on top of the snow. The area of the foot is now larger. The pressure is spread out so feet don't sink so easily.

Water exerts pressure, too. It grows greater as the water gets deeper. The water weight increases the pressure.

A force can accelerate or **decelerate** an object or change its direction. Speed also holds energy. The faster a moving object goes, the more energy it has. If a car crashes into another car, kinetic energy from the speed is changed to heat, sound, and mechanical energy. Those changes and damage are equal to the speed the car was going when it hit the other car.

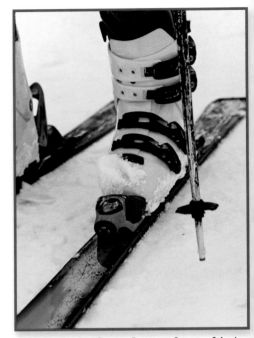

Gravity is the force that pushes a skier's mass down the slope. Skiers wax their skis to reduce friction and go faster.

The boat's force is greater than that of the pull by the skier, so it can lift the skier out of the water.

Centripetal force acts on an object to hold it toward the center. Think of a rollercoaster turning inside a loop. The motion energy tries to keep the cars going straight. But with a looped track, the cars are forced into a circle. The speed the coaster goes acts as the centripetal force to hold the riders inside the cars. If the coaster didn't go fast enough, the riders would fall out.

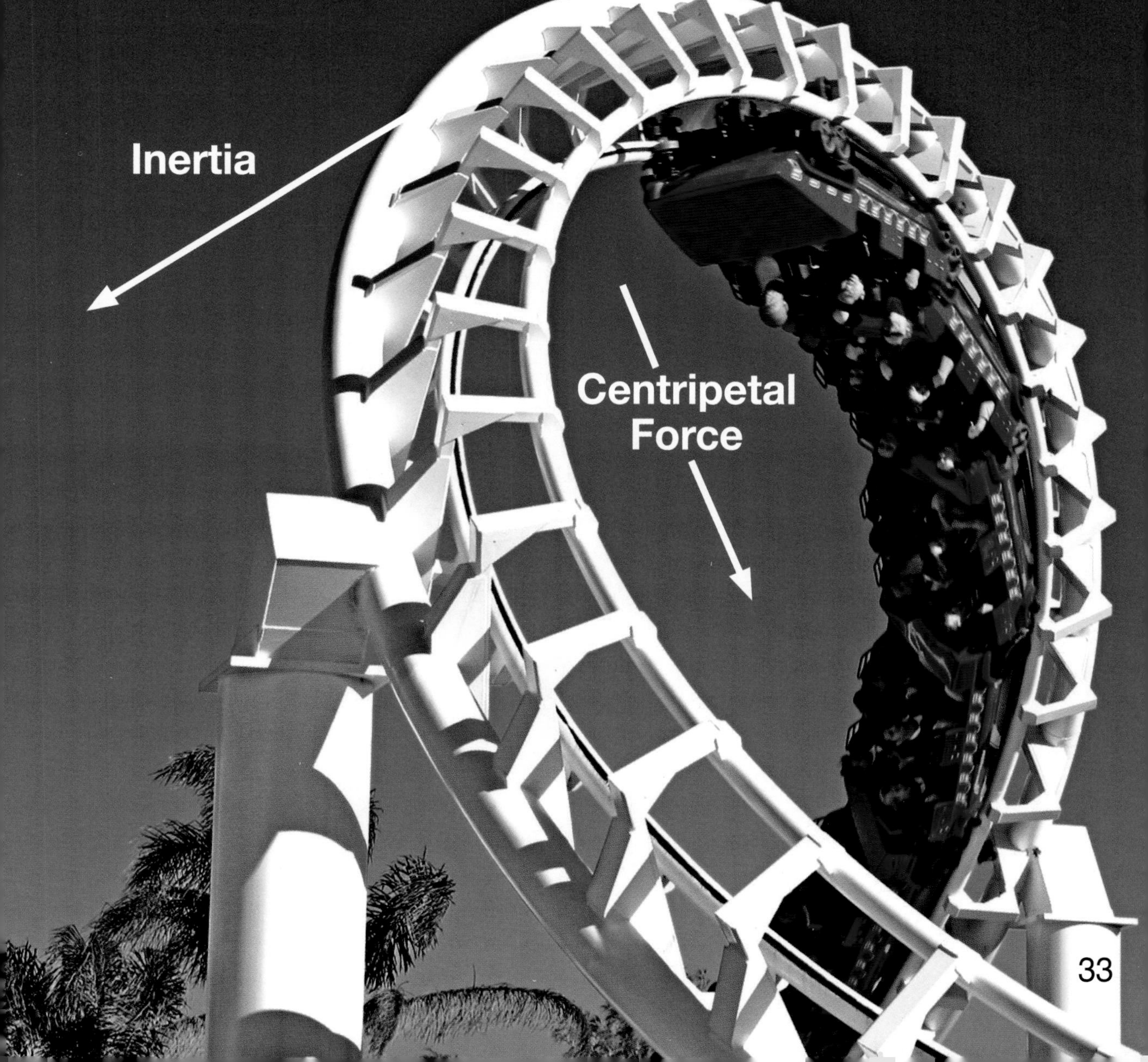

Inertia

Centripetal Force

Gravity is the centripetal force that keeps orbiting planets moving in a circular motion. The opposite motion is called **centrifugal force**. It isn't really a force. It's inertia. The bodies of the riders try to continue in a straight line. They feel their bodies resisting the effects of the motion as they turn. The chains prevent them from moving in a straight line.

On this ride, the bodies try to keep moving in a straight line because of inertia, but the force of the chains change the direction of the motion.

Elasticity is the property that causes an object or material to return to its original shape after being stretched or deformed.

Force acts on objects in other ways, too. Sturdy materials like rocks and metals can **deform**. They bend, stretch, or flatten under high pressure or heat. Other materials deform easily. Rubber or plastic can bend and stretch with little pressure.

Some deformable materials hold their shape after being deformed. Eyeglasses stretch to fit the wearer's face. The SillyBandz bracelets kids wear stretch to fit wrists, but the bracelets return to their shapes when removed. Materials that deform can only be stretched or bent so far. Too much stress will snap them.

CHAPTER FIVE

Energy at Work

People make forces work by using machines. Turning a doorknob may not seem like work. The force of a twist turns the knob a short distance. That makes the work of opening a door easier. Every day, people use machines to make work easier.

Machines help in two ways. Some change the amount of force needed. Others change the direction or distance of the force. Work becomes easier because smaller forces are exerted over longer distances.

The lever in this pump increases the force exerted and the pulley changes the direction of the force.

Simple Machines

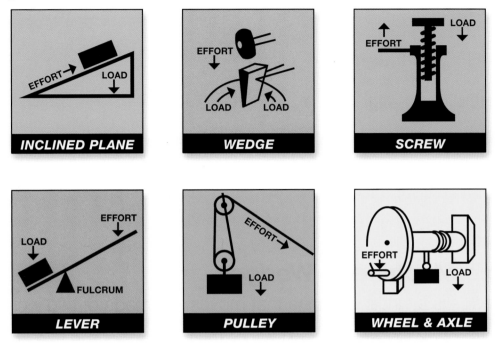

Simple Machines - Inclined Plane

Simple machines include the inclined plane, the wedge, the screw, the lever, the pulley, and the wheel and axle.

Imagine trying to lift a car onto a high platform. It's too heavy to pick up. Using a ramp makes the job easier. A ramp is an inclined plane, or a flat surface higher at one end. It reduces the amount of force needed to lift things. If the ramp is longer, it lessens how steep the ramp must be. The difference is that the car must move a longer distance. It's easier to move the car, but it must go further.

Rollercoasters, stairs, ladders, dump trucks, and boat propellers are all inclined planes. So are car windshields and funnels.

Wedge   *Screw*   *Inclined Plane*

Simple Machines - Wedges

A wedge is an inclined plane that moves. It's made of two inclined planes set back to back. To split a log, the user raises the axe and comes down with force. The thinner part of the wedge splits the wood.

Look at a key. The edges are a number of wedges. Each wedge on the key hits a pin inside the lock to open it. A zipper uses wedges to change a small force into a stronger one. Zipper teeth interlock and a wedge lets the pull lock or unlock the teeth with little effort.

Simple Machines - Screws

A screw is an inclined plane wrapped around a center core in a spiral. This shape allows a small turning force to act over a longer distance. Faucets, light bulbs, and jar lids use the screw to open and close. Electric fan blades, drills, and a nut and bolt work using a screw. The ridges in a screw are called threads.

Simple Machines - Levers

A lever helps lift a heavy load using the least amount of effort. A lever is a rigid bar that moves against a fixed point called a **fulcrum**. The lever swings against the fulcrum, which bears the weight. Levers are grouped by the position of the forces and the fulcrum. More distance on the lever requires less force to move the load, but the distance is greater. The user pulls or pushes against the lever to increase the force.

Three Classes of Levers

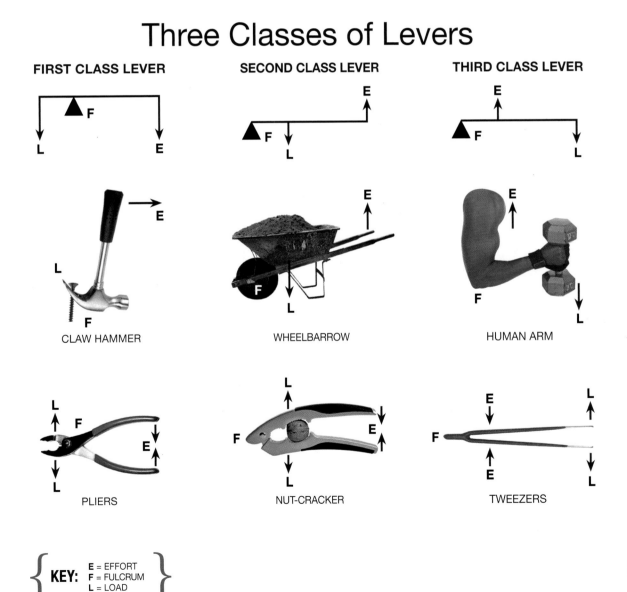

FIRST CLASS LEVER	SECOND CLASS LEVER	THIRD CLASS LEVER
CLAW HAMMER	WHEELBARROW	HUMAN ARM
PLIERS	NUT-CRACKER	TWEEZERS

{ **KEY:** E = EFFORT F = FULCRUM L = LOAD }

Simple Machines - Pulleys

A pulley is a rope or belt wrapped around a grooved wheel. A pulley changes the amount of force or the direction of a force. Pulleys can be fixed to stay in one place. A fixed pulley changes the direction of the force. A flagpole holds a fixed pulley. By pulling down, the flag, or load, moves up.

A movable pulley attaches to the load so it can hold or support the load it's moving. Two examples of movable pulleys are a crane and zip lines.

Simple Machines - Wheels and Axles

The wheel and axle is a simple machine made of two different-sized circular objects. The wheel is the larger circle and the axle is smaller. The force is applied to the wheel, which turns the axle. The wheel moves a greater distance, but the force is increased on the turning axle. Windmills, bicycle wheels, rolling pins, Ferris wheels, pencil sharpeners, and steering wheels are examples of wheels and axles.

Gears are another form of the wheel and axle. Gears have interlocking teeth. They change a small turning force into a larger one. Gears also transmit force over a distance.

Both of the chains on this pulley are lifting the load, so they divide the load in two. Each chain lifts half of the weight, making the work easier.

When gears are connected, or meshing, a gear with more teeth will turn with more force.
The second gear will turn faster, but with less force.

Bicycling uphill is easier using a low gear. The biker turns the pedals at the same rate, but the wheels turn more slowly. The turning force is called **torque**. Clocks, bicycles, and cars use gears to help them run.

Compound Machines

Compound machines combine two or more simple machines. Bicycles, watches, blenders, can openers, and cars are compound machines. Many of the machines people use every day are compound machines. Machines make work easier to do. However, the work the machine does is always equal to the amount of work put into a machine.

Machines use forces to make life easier and more convenient. People use forces, energy, and machines in many different ways.

CHAPTER SIX

Using Forces and Motion

All energy is either renewable or nonrenewable. Renewable energy sources include solar, wind, geothermal, biomass, and hydropower. Solar energy comes from the Sun. Special panels absorb the Sun's light energy and convert it to electricity. Plants also convert the Sun's energy. They change sunlight into energy to create food.

Wind energy is captured by turning **turbines** on wind farms. The wind makes the blades spin and the mechanical energy is changed to electricity. This energy depends on the strength and constancy of the wind.

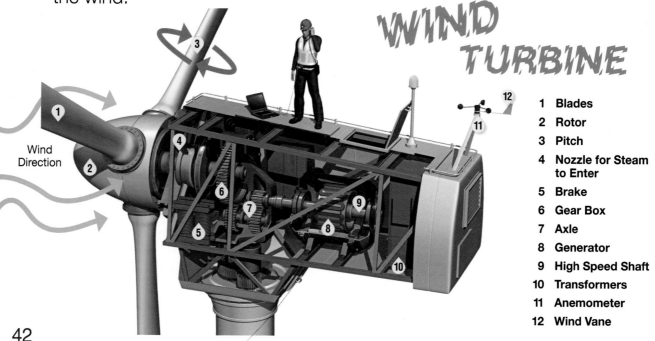

WIND TURBINE

Wind Direction

1   Blades
2   Rotor
3   Pitch
4   Nozzle for Steam to Enter
5   Brake
6   Gear Box
7   Axle
8   Generator
9   High Speed Shaft
10 Transformers
11 Anemometer
12 Wind Vane

Geothermal energy uses the heat deep inside the Earth. Heated rocks and water far below the surface make steam. The steam is piped up and turns a turbine. A turbine is a wheel with blades and an axle connected to a generator. The turning generator changes the motion energy into usable electricity.

Geothermal Energy

Biomass is energy from plants. Burning firewood from trees converts to heat. Trees can be replanted. Corn makes ethanol, a kind of fuel. Vegetable oil can also be used to make fuel. Using food sources for energy could lead to higher food prices. Certain waste materials make biogas. It comes from manure, decaying leaves, and other plant matter.

Biomass

Hydropower comes from moving water. Dams create a place for water to drop. This motion moves a turbine, which spins to change motion into electricity.

Hydropower

Nonrenewable fuel resources are coal, oil, and gas. These fossil fuels developed underground long ago. Burning these fuels converts the stored energy to heat.

Heat energy provides warmth and security. People cook food using heat energy. Chemical energy provides power for electricity or when cooking food. Burning fuels provide this energy.

Electrical energy supplies power to run household appliances, tools, and lights. Nuclear energy provides power for homes and has also been used for weapon making and defense systems.

Total Consumption by Source
Percentage of Energy Resources Used

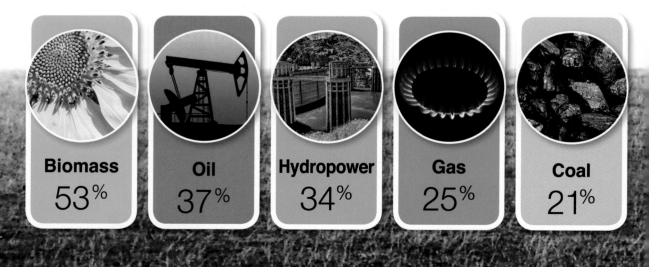

Biomass	Oil	Hydropower	Gas	Coal
53%	37%	34%	25%	21%

Light energy can heat homes, warm water, or be converted into electricity.

Sound energy keeps people safe. Sirens blast warnings from fire trucks or ambulances or sound tornado warnings. Sound energy makes entertainment. Listening to music, talking on the phone, or playing an instrument uses sound.

The world would be a different place without the forces of nature and motion. Understanding the laws that run the world allow people to better understand the world we live in. People can use these predictable laws to improve their lives and learn more about their own world and worlds beyond.

Nuclear 09% **Renewable** 08% **Wind** 07% **Geothermal** 05% **Solar** 01%

Glossary

aerodynamics (air-oh-dye-NAM-iks): the study of how air flows

centrifugal force (sen-TRIF-yuh-guhl forss): tending to move away from the center

centripetal force (sen-TRIP-uh-tuhl forss): tending to move toward the center

decelerate (dee-SEL-uh-rate): to slow something down using a force

deform (di-FORM): bend, stretch, or flatten something

electromagnet (i-lek-troh-MAG-nit): a magnet created by using electricity to move charged particles through a coil of wire around a piece of iron that stops being a magnet when the current is disconnected

forces (FORS-ez): actions that start, stop, or change the shape or motion of a body

fulcrum (FUL-kruhm): a fixed point on which a lever rests or moves

gravity (GRAV -i- tee): unseen force holding the universe together by attraction between any two objects

inertia (in-UR-shuh): the tendency of an object to keep moving or to stay at rest

kinetic energy (ki-NET-ik EN-ur-jee): energy in motion

magnets (MAG-nitz): metals that attract iron and other metals to it with a force field of moving particles

mass (mass): the amount of matter in something

mechanics (muh-KAN-iks): the study of forces and motion

natural philosophers (NACH-ur-uhl fuh-LOSS-suh-fuhrs): early scientists

nuclear forces (NOO-klee-ur FORS-ez): forces created by atoms and the particles that make them

potential energy (puh-TEN-shuhl EN-ur-jee): stored energy or energy of position

resistance (ri-ZISS-tuhnss): any force opposing the motion of another object

torque (tork): a turning force

turbines (TUR-buhnz): wheels with blades and an axle connected to a generator which turns to make electricity

weight (wate): the force with which gravity pulls down on an object

work (wurk): the amount of energy necessary for a force to change an object's motion

Index

Wesites to Visit

www.teachertech.rice.edu/Participants/louviere/Newton/

www.eia.doe.gov/kids/

www.neok12.com/Laws-of-Motion.htm

About the Author

Shirley Duke enjoys science and books. She studied biology and education at Austin College in Texas. Then she taught science in elementary, middle, and high school for many years. Her favorite lesson to teach was simple machines. Using her science background, she changed careers and now writes books for young people. In addition to a picture book and a young adult book, her first two science books are You Can't Wear These Genes and Infections, Infestations, and Diseases in the Let's Explore Science series. Visit Shirley at www.shirleysmithduke.com or www.simplyscience.wordpress.com.